Dedicated

To

All the Past & Present Judges of the Supreme Court of India.

Salute to their wisdom.

Salute to their interpretation of Law.

Salute to their elaborative judgement writing.

Dedicated

To

All the Past & Present Judges of the Supreme Court of India

Salute to their wisdom,

Salute to their interpretation of Law

Salute to their elaborative judgement writing

SENIORITY-SERVICE MATTER-SUPREME COURT'S LATEST LEADING CASE LAWS

CASE NOTES- FACTS- FINDINGS OF APEX COURT JUDGES & CITATIONS

JAYPRAKASH BANSILAL SOMANI

ISBN 979-888569607-4

Contents

Contents

Preface

Dear Learned Advocates of the Trial Courts, Tribunals, Appellate Tribunals, High Courts, Supreme Court, HR Professionals, Corporates, Govt Recruitment Officers & Employees,

I am very delighted to provide you a book on 'Seniority- Service Matter - Supreme Court of India's Latest Leading Case Laws'.

In this book you will get...

1. Name of the Case i. e. Cause title

2.Relevant Sections discussed in the case

3.Hon'ble Judges/Coram of the case

4.Number of PDF Pages in Original Judgement of the case

5. All available Citations of the case

6. Case Note with appeal allowed/ dismissed or disposed off

7. Facts of the case

8.Hon'ble Apex Court's findings, while dismissing/allowing or disposing the appeal

9. Ratio Decidendi if any.

My special thanks to Manupatra, because of their web portal I can compile this book in well manner. I am also thankful to Notion Press to support me to publish & market this book throughout the Country. Thanks to my Juniors, Advocate Colleagues & Insolvency Professional Colleagues to support me in this venture.

Miss Devpriya Shah has helped me a lot to compile this book.

I hope this book will add some value addition in the wealth of your legal knowledge. Your positive feedbacks will boost me to compile/ write further books & negative feedbacks will improve my skills. Kindly send your valuable feedbacks by email.

Thanks with Regards,

Jayprakash B. Somani

Advocate, Supreme Court of India

Email: jaysomani64@gmail.com

Web Site:www.jayprakashsomani.com

Call: 8384051134, 9322188701, 9318381287

Acknowledgements

Printed & Published by

Notion Press

No. 8, 3rd Cross Street,

CIT Colony, Mylapore,

Chennai, Tamil Nadu- 600004

ꝒꝒꝒ

Managed by

Jayprakash Somani Advocates & Solicitors

Law Firm for Supreme Court of India

Delhi Office

257 C, Pocket 1, Mayur Vihar Phase 1, Delhi 110091.

Call 8384051134, 9322188701, 8459194576, 01141051516

Supreme Court Chamber

312, 3rd Floor, M. C. Setalvad Block, In front of 'D' Gate, Bhagwan Das Road, Supreme Court of India, New Delhi 110001

Contact: 8459194576, 9811011747

www.jayprakashsomani.com

ꝒꝒꝒ

Books are available online at

1. Notion Press: https://notionpress.com/author/jayprakash_somani

2. Amazon: https://www.amazon.in/s?k=jayprakash+somani

3. Flipkart: https://www.flipkart.com/search?q=Jayprakash%20Somani

ꝒꝒꝒ

ONE

SUDHIR KUMAR ATREY VS. UNION OF INDIA (UOI) AND ORS., 2021

Hon'ble Judges/Coram:

Ajay Rastogi and Abhay Shreeniwas Oka, JJ.

Equivalent Citation: 2021(4)SCT385(SC), MANU/SC/0987/2021

Relevant Section/provisions: Military Engineering Service (Non-Industrial Class III and IV Posts) Rules, 1971

Number of Pages in the Original Judgment: 07

Case Note:

Service - Seniority - Promotion - Determination thereof - Military Engineering Service (Non-Industrial Class III and IV Posts) Rules, 1971 (1971 Rules) - No rules in place to determine seniority - Whether revision made in seniority list rightly determined?

Brief Facts:

The Military Engineering Service for administrative purposes was bifurcated into five Commands being the Eastern, Western, Northern, Southern and the Central Command with an officer of the rank of Chief Engineer being the administrative head and controller of each Command. The service conditions are governed by the 1971 Rules. There was no provision under the Scheme of 1971 Rules or guidelines to govern seniority of persons appointed in their respective Commands. The Office Memorandum dated 3rd July, 1986 issued laid down the principles for determination of seniority of persons appointed to service on posts in Central Government, of direct recruits and promotees of one and the same select panel, seniority of transferees and those who were recruited in special type of cases. The Tribunal observed that while adjudging seniority in such situation the only possibility and rationale Rule would be to have their seniority reckoned from the date of entering into service when compared to the person who belonged to yet another Command. In such background present issue requiring adjudication of seniority came up.

Held, while dismissing the Appeal:

i. It is not disputed that there is no Rule or guidelines issued by the Respondents which may determine the inter se seniority when a combined seniority list at the All India level is to be prepared under the Scheme of 1971 Rules and the Respondents were taking assistance of Office Memorandum of DoPT dated 3rd July, 1986 which deals with the determination of seniority of direct recruits who were selected and placed in one and the same select panel to be determined by the order of merit in the select list and those who are selected in the earlier selection shall remain senior to such persons who were appointed in the later selection and also with regard to relative seniority of direct recruits vis-o?=-vis the promotees in the cadre.

ii. When all the five Commands have initiated the process of selection independently at the same time pursuant to the directives of the Engineer-in-Chief, Army Headquarters, the principle of initial date of appointment/ continuous officiation may be the valid principle to be considered for determination of inter se seniority in the absence of any Rule or guidelines to the contrary keeping in view the principles laid down by the Constitution Bench in Direct Recruit Class II Engineering Officers' Association v. State of Maharashtra and Ors

iii. Since the seniority list of the Respondents in Civil Appeal @ SLP (C) No. 5275 of 2021 was revised pursuant to the judgment impugned, although the principles laid down have not been approved by this Court, but the fact remains that both the incumbents were promoted in terms of their revised seniority to the higher promotional post and one of them had retired from service in October 2018 and the other incumbent is at the verge of retirement in March 2022, in these peculiar circumstances, this Court in exercise of its power under Article 142 of the Constitution to do complete justice is not inclined to disturb the seniority which has been assigned to them in compliance with the order of the Tribunal although on principle has not been accepted/approved.

TWO

MALOOK SINGH AND ORS. VS.: STATE OF PUNJAB AND ORS., 2021

Hon'ble Judges/Coram:

Dr. D.Y. Chandrachud, Vikram Nath and B.V. Nagarathna, JJ.

Equivalent Citation: 2021(4)SCT305(SC), 2021(3)SLJ377(SC), MANU/SC/0795/2021

Relevant Section/provisions: Rule 9 of the Punjab Civil Secretariat (State Service Class III) Rules 1976; Article 226 of the Constitution of India

Number of Pages in the Original Judgment: 04

Case Note:

Service - Seniority - Determination thereof - Ad hoc appointees - Pensionary benefits -Recovery thereof - Whether the period of ad hoc service can be counted for the purpose of determining seniority?

Brief Facts:

Appellants were appointed as clerks in 1975-1976 on ad hoc basis. On 3 May 1977, their services were regularized with effect from 1/4/1977.Issue involved in the present matter was determination of seniority of those regularised after they were initially appointed on ad hoc basis and grant of pensionary benefits.

Held, while dismissing the Appeal:

i. Revising the seniority at this length of time would cast an insuperable burden on the State. During the pendency of these proceedings, an exercise was directed to be conducted on a limited basis, for which several months were required. Retrieving correct data to rework seniority commencing from April 1977 would be extremely difficult, resulting in further litigation. With this backdrop, when most of the pensioners have retired from service several years ago, it would be in the interests of justice if the pensionary benefits which they are now receiving are duly protected both against recoveries and in respect of their disbursement for the future. Such a direction would be manifestly in the interest of justice. Insofar as the private Respondents are concerned, they too like the Appellants have been promoted from time to time during the pendency of these proceedings since 2011 and are in the receipt of pensionary benefits. The mattermust rest there so that the pensioners are not left in a state of uncertainty at this stage of their lives after rendering long years of service to the State in the Punjab Civil Secretariat.

ii. The pensionary benefits which are being disbursed to the Appellants shall not be disturbed. No recoveries shall be made of any nature whatsoever from the Appellants. No further directions are required in the companion appeals.

PPP

THREE

Anand Kumar Tiwari and Ors. Vs. High Court of Madhya Pradesh and Ors., 2021

Hon'ble Judges/Coram:

L. Nageswara Rao and Aniruddha Bose, JJ.

Equivalent Citation: Equivalent Citation: AIR2021SC3898, 2021(3)JLJ611, 2021LabIC3228, 2021(3)SCT596(SC), 2021(3)SLJ19(SC), MANU/SC/0525/2021

Relevant Section/provisions: Rule 11 of the Madhya Pradesh Higher Judicial Services (Recruitment and Conditions of Service) Rules, 2017

Number of Pages in the Original Judgment: 05

Case Note:

Service - Interse seniority - Quashing of Amendment and order determining inter-se seniority-Madhya Pradesh Uchchtar Nyayik Sewa (Bharti Tatha Seva Sharten) Niyam, 1994 -- Direct recruited and promotee District Judges through Limited Competitive Examination (LCE)- Quashing Rule 11 of the Madhya Pradesh Higher Judicial Services (Recruitment and Conditions of Service) Rules, 2017 (2017 Rules) - 2017 Rules further also sought to be given retrospective effect - Whether reliefs as sought could be granted to the Petitioners?

Brief Facts:

The present petitions were filed to challenge order effecting promotion of direct recruits. Order was passed pursuant to representation made by promotee District Judges as a result of which direct recruits were shown lower in the seniority list. Hence, the present petitions on the primary issue to determine basis of seniority.

Held, while dismissing the Appeals:

i. Realising that the principle of continuous officiation is well settled, especially where inter-se seniority is not dealt with in the Rules, the Full Court of the High Court correctly approved the resolution of the Special Committee. After the introduction of the 2017 Rules, seniority inter-se direct recruits and promotees shall be determined on the basis of Roster

ii. Main issues since answered against the Petitioners, it is not necessary to deal with the other submissions made on their behalf. Writ Petitions dismissed.

ÞÞÞ

FOUR

Prem Narayan Singh and Ors. Vs. Hon'ble High Court of Madhya Pradesh, 2021

Hon'ble Judges/Coram:

L. Nageswara Rao and Aniruddha Bose, JJ.

Equivalent Citation: AIR2021SC3892, 2021(3)JLJ601, 2021LabIC3263, (2021)7SCC649, 2021(3)SCT592(SC), 2021(3)SLJ53(SC), MANU/SC/0526/2021

Relevant Section/provisions: Madhya Pradesh Higher Judicial Services (Recruitment and Conditions of Service) Rules, 1994

Number of Pages in the Original Judgment: 06

Case Note:

Service - Seniority - Inter se - Determination thereof - Judicial Service - Madhya Pradesh Higher Judicial Services (Recruitment and Conditions of Service) Rules, 1994 (1994 Rules) - Rule 11(1) of the Madhya Pradesh Higher Judicial Services (Recruitment and Conditions of Service) Rules, 2017 (2017 Rules) - Whether seniority as District Judges properly fixed in accordance with the settled position?

Brief Facts:

The Petitioners are Members of the Higher Judicial Services working as District Judges in the State of Madhya Pradesh. They were selected in the Limited Competitive Examinations (LCE). They have challenged the resolution of Administrative Committee of the High Court by which it resolved that the merit of candidates in LCE would not be relevant for altering inter se seniority in the feeder cadre. The Full Court resolution, revised gradation list on the basis of the resolution also questioned in the Writ Petition. Thus, in any event, 50 per cent of the posts of District Judges was to be filled by promotion on the principle of merit-cum-seniority. The dispute in this case concerned with seniority inter se amongst those who were promoted through LCE.

Held, while dismissing the Appeals:

i. Inter se placement of candidates selected through LCE must be based on merit and not on the basis of seniority in the erstwhile cadre.
ii. The reason for introduction of promotion through LCE is to improve the calibre of the members of Higher Judicial Services. Such of those meritorious candidates who have been promoted on the basis of LCE cannot be deprived of their seniority on the basis of merit in the examination.
iii. Rule 11(1) of the 2017 Rules makes it clear that the relative seniority of members of the service who are holding substantive posts at the time of commencement of the Rules shall be as it existed before the commencement of the Rules. The seniority of the Petitioners which has been determined prior to the 2017 Rules cannot be disturbed. The Petitioners will not be adversely affected by Rule 11(4)(b) of the 2017 Rules which alters the criteria for determination of seniority from merit to inter se seniority in the lower cadre.Writ Petition allowed.

FIVE

Rashi Mani Mishra and Ors. Vs.: State of Uttar Pradesh and Ors., 2021

Hon'ble Judges/Coram:

Dr. D.Y. Chandrachud and M.R. Shah, JJ.

Equivalent Citation: 2021(7)ADJ591, 2021 (148) ALR 371, 2021(5)BLJ84, [2021(171)FLR328], 2021(3)SCT518(SC), 2021(3)SLJ1(SC), MANU/SC/0484/2021

Relevant Section/provisions: Uttar Pradesh Regularisation of Ad hoc Appointments (on posts within the purview of the Public Service Commission) Rules, 1979; Rules 3(g), 3(i) and Rule 21 of Uttar Pradesh Rural Engineering (Group 'B') Service Rules, 1993

Number of Pages in the Original Judgment: 14

Case Note:

Service - Determination of Seniority - Ad hoc employee subsequently regularised - Uttar Pradesh Regularisation of Ad hoc Appointments (on posts within the purview of the Public Service Commission) Rules, 1979 - Uttar Pradesh Regularisation of Ad hoc Appointments (on posts within the purview of the Public Service Commission) (Second Amendment) Rules, 1989 (1989 Rules) - Whether services rendered as ad hoc prior to regularisation to be counted to determine seniority etc. or from the date of regularisation?

Brief Facts:

In the instant case, 108 Assistant Engineers were given ad hoc appointments in the year 1985 and were subsequently regularised in the year 1989. Services rendered by such Assistant Engineers on ad hoc basis were not counted for seniority purposes and their seniority was determined from the date of their regularisation. In previous challenges reaching upto Apex Court, it was held that services rendered by Assistant Engineers as ad hoc would be counted for the purpose of seniority to be counted from the date of their initial appointment and not from the date of regularisation of their services. This Court directed State to redetermine the seniority after hearing the affected parties. It was clarified that benefit of re-determination of seniority at this stage would not disturb holding of posts by any incumbent and except for the benefit in pension other benefits to which the writ Petitioner may be found entitled would be given only on notional basis. Thereafter state government issued office order notifying the tentative seniority list and after considering objections, a final seniority list was published. The writ Petitioners before the High Court were the candidates who were downgraded in the seniority list. High Court by the impugned judgment set aside the plea seeking setting aside of list.

Held, while dismissing the Appeals:

i. As per the 1979 Rules, the persons whose services have been regularised and they are appointed after the recommendations by the Selection Committee as per the 1979 Rules, their seniority shall be only from the date of order of appointment after selection in accordance with the 1979 Rules, i.e., in the present case, from 23.02.1989.
ii. It is also required to be noted that neither in the year 1985 when they were appointed on ad hoc basis on temporary posts nor at the time when their services were regularised in the year 1989, the service Rules for Group 'B' were in force. In the year 1993, Uttar Pradesh Rural Engineering (Group 'B') Service Rules, 1993 came to be enacted. Rules 3(g), 3(i) and Rule 21. As per Rule 21 of the 1993 Rules, the seniority of persons substantively appointed to a post in the service shall be determined in accordance with the Uttar Pradesh Government Servants' Seniority Rules, 1991, as amended from time to time. Even as per the Service Rules, 1993, "substantive appointment" means an appointment, not being an ad hoc appointment, on a post in the cadre of the service..... As per Seniority Rules, 1991, which also defines the "substantive appointment" as per Rule 4(h), the seniority shall be counted only from the date of their

"substantive appointment". In the present case, Seniority Rules clearly provide that seniority in any category or cadre post shall be determined from the date of order of "substantive appointment".

iii. Services rendered by the ad hoc appointees prior to their regularisation as per the 1979 Rules shall not be counted for the purpose of seniority, vis-o?=-vis, the direct recruits who were appointed prior to 1989 and they are not entitled to seniority from the date of their initial appointment in the year 1985. The resultant effect would be that the subsequent re-determination of the seniority in the year 2016 cannot be sustained which was considering the services rendered by ad hoc appointees prior to 1989, i.e., from the date of their initial appointment in 1985.

iv. In view of the above and for the reasons stated above, all the appeals succeed. The re-determination of the seniority and the revised seniority list dated 22.03.2016 counting the services of the ad hoc appointees prior to 23.02.1989 and counting the services as ad hoc from 12.06.1985 for the purpose of seniority is hereby quashed and set aside and the final seniority list dated 14.12.2001 fixing the seniority considering the services rendered by ad hoc appointees from 23.02.1989 is hereby restored.

ÞÞÞ

SIX

JAGMOHAN SINGH DHILLON AND ORS. VS. SATWANT SINGH AND ORS., 2021

Hon'ble Judges/Coram:

Ashok Bhushan, S. Abdul Nazeer and Hemant Gupta, JJ.

Equivalent Citation: AIR2021SC2001, 2021(3)ALT52, 2021LabIC2321, 2021(2)SCT172(SC), (2021)2UPLBEC1406, MANU/SC/0230/2021

Relevant Section/provisions: Sections 4 and 4(1) of Demobilized Indian Armed Forces Personnel Rules, 1972

Number of Pages in the Original Judgment: 07

Case Note:

Service - Seniority - Fixation of - Sections 4 and 4(1) of Demobilized Indian Armed Forces Personnel Rules, 1972 - Appellants were ex-servicemen, who after being released from Army were appointed to Punjab Civil Service (Executive Branch) - Advertisement was published for post of Punjab Civil Service (Executive Branch) and examination was held in which Appellants were appointed - Seniority list was issued in which seniority of Appellant was fixed without granting him any benefit of earlier services in Army - Appellant submitted representation against wrong fixation of his seniority - Appellant filed Writ Petition claimed that his seniority be re-fixed by granting military services benefit in terms of Rule 4 of 1972 Rules - Single Judge of High Court allowed writ petition holding that Appellants shall be deemed to be appointed under 1972 Rules and benefits flowing there from shall be admissible to the Appellant as per 1972 Rules - Aggrieved against judgment of Single Judge, appeal was preferred before Division Bench in which order of Single Judge was set aside - Hence, present appeal - Whether Appellant for determination of his seniority was entitled for benefit of Rule 4 of 1972 Rules.

Brief Facts:

The Appellants were ex-servicemen, who after being released from the Army were appointed to Punjab Civil Service (Executive Branch). An advertisement was published advertising the post of Punjab Civil Service (Executive Branch). The examination was held and the Appellants were appointed to Punjab Civil Service (Executive Branch). The seniority list was issued in which seniority of the Appellant was fixed without granting him any benefit of earlier services in the Army. The Appellant submitted representation against wrong fixation of his seniority. The Appellant filed a Writ Petition. In the writ petition, the Appellant claimed that his seniority be re-fixed by granting military services benefit in terms of Rule 4 of 1972 Rules. The writ petition of the Appellant was taken along with other three writ petitions and allowed by Single Judge of the High Court. The Single Judge held that Appellants shall be deemed to be appointed under 1972 Rules and benefits flowing there from shall be admissible to the Appellant as per 1972 Rules. Aggrieved against the judgment of Single Judge, State preferred appeal before the Division Bench. LPA filed by the State was allowed and judgment of the Single Judge was set aside.

Held, while dismissing the appeal:

i. It was clear that the advertisement against which the Appellant was appointed was issued after the enforcement of 1982 Rules. The Appellant was appointed in pursuance of the advertisement by appointment order. Although 1972 Rules had been repealed but in the 1982 Rules, as per Rule 9(3), nothing in 1982 Rules was to be construed as depriving any person of any right which had accrued under the Rules in force immediately before the commencement of the Rules 1982. Before enforcement of 1982 Rules admittedly, 1972 Rules were enforced.

ii. 1982 Rules specifically repealed the 1972 Rules, thus, the Rule 4 of 1972 Rules which provided for benefit of seniority of Army service was no longer entitled to be counted for seniority for personnel who was appointed after enforcement of 1982 Rules. The judgment of Ishwar

Singh of High Court which only determined the percentage of reserved vacancies which were to be reserved for Army personnel could not be held to be relevant regarding determination of seniority in the facts of the present case.

iii. Under 1982 Rules, there was no indication that the benefit which was available to Armed Forces Personnel Under Rule 4 of 1972 Rules were continued or any right had been accrued on the Appellant under 1972 Rules which he was entitled to avail regarding seniority.

iv. The Division Bench had rightly taken the view that saving Clause under Rule 9(3) did not extend any benefit to the Appellant since there was nothing to show that any right of weightage for army services for seniority has already accrued before he joined services. Saving Clause in Rule 9(3) could not be availed by the Appellant. Thus, fully endorse the above view of the Division Bench taken in the impugned order.

v. Thus, the Appellant was not entitled to claim benefit of military service for purpose of seniority for appointment to Punjab Civil Service (Executive Branch) since the benefit of Rule 4(1) of 1972 Rules was not continued in 1982 Rules. His seniority was to be governed by statutory Rules applicable after the enforcement of 1982 Rules.

SEVEN

VINOD PRASAD RATURI AND ORS. VS. UNION OF INDIA (UOI) AND ORS., 2021

Hon'ble Judges/Coram:

L. Nageswara Rao and S. Ravindra Bhat, JJ.

Equivalent Citation: 2021(5)ADJ305, AIR2021SC1264, 2021(2)ESC392(SC), [2021(169)FLR495], 2021(2)SCT73(SC), 2021(2)SLJ10(SC), 2021(3)SLR646(SC)

Relevant Section/provisions: Uttar Pradesh Reorganization Act, 2000

Number of Pages in the Original Judgment: 07

Case Note:

Service -Promotion - Seniority List - Indian Administrative Services (IAS) cadre- Review - Departmental Promotion Committee (DPC)-Reorganisation of State of Uttar Pradesh - Respondent No. 4 allotted to State of Uttarakhand - Revision of seniority list sought by R4 upon his junior given promotion ahead of him - High Court directed revision - Hence, the present appeal - Whether such direction as passed sustainable when passed without Appellants being heard?

Brief Facts:

Pursuant to the Uttar Pradesh Reorganization Act, 2000 (Act), the State of Uttarakhand was created. The Central Government issued guidelines for allocation of erstwhile employees of the State of Uttar Pradesh amongst the two States. Allocations as per seniority list prepared directed. Respondent

No. 4 amongst others were also allocated to the State of Uttarakhand. The request made by the Government of Uttar Pradesh for retention of Respondent No. 4 in the State of Uttar Pradesh was rejected by the Central Government. Respondent No. 4 was relieved from Uttar Pradesh and thereafter, he joined the services of the State of Uttarakhand. Respondent No. 4 was promoted to IAS on 09.01.2018 and allocated the year of allotment as 2010. As his juniors were given the year of allotment from 2005 onwards, Respondent No. 4 requested for revision of his seniority in the IAS cadre and accordingly requested for a review DPC. On this issue, High Court disposed his Writ Petition with direction to the Respondents to hold a review DPC. Hence, the present appeal. The Appellants contended that the High Court committed an error in directing the review DPC to be conducted without hearing them.

Held, while allowing the Appeals:

Respondent No. 4 cannot be permitted to seek review of the promotions made while he was serving the State of Uttar Pradesh. The promotion of the Appellants cannot be disturbed by the 4th Respondent who continued to work in Uttar Pradesh of his volition. The High Court committed an error in directing a review DPC to be conducted without hearing the affected parties and without realising that there was a likelihood of seniority of other officers being disturbed. Judgment of the High Court is set aside and the Appeal is allowed.

EIGHT

A. Rajagopalan and Ors. Vs. The District Collector, Thiruchirapalli District and Ors., 2019

Hon'ble Judges/Coram:

R. Banumathi and R. Subhash Reddy, JJ.

Equivalent Citation: 2019(1)ESC243(SC), 2019(4)LLN289(SC), 2019(5)SCALE79, (2019)5SCC560, 2019(2)SCT231(SC), 2019(1)SLJ425(SC), 2019(6)SLR162(SC), MANU/SC/0357/2019

Relevant Section/provisions: Rule 5(g) of Tamil Nadu Revenue Subordinate Service Rules

Number of Pages in the Original Judgment: 08

Case Note:

Service - Seniority list - Validity of - Amendment made to Rule 5(g) of Tamil Nadu Revenue Subordinate Service Rules by which Assistant appointed by direct recruitment completed total service of five years, shall be eligible for inclusion of his name in approved list of Deputy Tahsildars - Tribunal set aside said amendment on application filed by Promotee Assistants - High Court set aside order of Tribunal - Aggrieved by order of High Court, appeal filed whereby Supreme Court upheld validity of the amendment to Rule 5(g) - Accordingly, District Collectors redrawing seniority list by treating Direct recruit Assistants on par with Promotee graduate Assistants - Writ petitions were filed, praying to stay orders of redrawal of seniority list which was dismissed by Single Judge - On appeal, Division Bench directed Respondents to draw seniority list taking Direct recruit Assistants, Promotee graduate Assistants and Promotee non-graduate Assistants as one group - Hence, present appeal - Whether impugned direction of Division Bench pertaining to seniority list warrant any interference.

Brief Facts:

The Direct recruit Assistants in Revenue Department submitted representation that they be given preferential treatment in the matter of promotion to the cadre of Deputy Tahsildar without basing their seniority in the Assistant list. Amendment made to Rule 5(g) of the TNRSS by which Assistant appointed by direct recruitment in the office of the erstwhile Board of Revenue, who had completed a total service of five years, shall be eligible for inclusion of his name in the approved list of Deputy Tahsildars. Promotee Assistants challenged the said amendment before Tribunal which was set aside by the Tribunal. The High Court set aside the order of the Tribunal. Aggrieved by the order of the High Court, Promotee Assistants filed appeal before the Supreme Court whereby the Supreme Court upheld the validity of the amendment to Rule 5(g) of TNRSS Rules to the extent that it gives preference to the Direct recruit Assistants over the Promotee non-graduate Assistants. Accordingly, the District Collectors had passed orders redrawing the seniority list by treating the Direct recruit Assistants on par with the Promotee graduate Assistants and redrawn the panel of Deputy Tahsildars and this had effected the seniority of number of Direct recruit Assistants. Being aggrieved by the orders of the District Collectors, a batch of writ petitions were filed by the Promotee non-graduate Assistants, praying to stay the orders of redrawal of the seniority list. The Single Judge dismissed the writ petitions. The High Court had set aside the order of the Single Judge and directed the Respondents to draw the seniority list taking Direct recruit Assistants, Promotee graduate Assistants and Promotee non-graduate Assistants as one group for promotion as Deputy Tahsildar.

Held, while allowing the appeal:

i. The Division Bench did not keep in view that the letter by which the government accepted the proposal directed to take non-graduate promotees along with graduate promotees and direct recruits as one group, was still only a proposal and the Rules were yet to be amended. The Division Bench fell in error by relying upon the said letter and erred in directing the State to treat the Promotee non-graduate Assistants, Promotee graduate Assistants and Direct recruit Assistants as one category and draw revised seniority list for the purpose of promotion to the post of Deputy Tahsildar. The Division Bench failed to notice that the amendment to Rule 5(g) of TNRSS Rules had been upheld by the Supreme Court and had attained finality. The direction of the Division Bench to treat all three categories viz. Promotee non-graduate Assistants, Promotee graduate Assistants and Direct recruit Assistants as one group for the promotion to the post of Deputy Tahsildar virtually amounts to reversing the judgment of the Supreme Court. The direction of the Division Bench in the impugned judgment was wholly misconceived.

ii. The amendment to Rule 5(g) of TNRSS Rules had been upheld by the Supreme Court, of course, by reading down into the Rule that the Promotee graduate Assistants were to be treated on par with Direct recruit Assistants. The classification of the Promotee graduate Assistants on par with Direct recruit Assistants was only by virtue of the order of the Supreme Court. The implementation of the order would create unprecedented confusion and upset the settled position of Direct recruit Assistants who had been promoted by virtue of the amended Rule conferring preferential treatment on the Direct recruit Assistants. If such a course of action was permitted, it would seriously prejudice the rights of those of the Direct recruit Assistants who had been promoted.

iii. By wrongly relying on the letter of the Government, in the impugned judgment, the High Court had held that graduate and non-graduate Promotee Assistants would be considered as one single category along with Assistants and the impugned judgment of the High Court could not be sustained and was liable to be set aside.

iv. Thus, the impugned judgment of the High Court was set aside with directions that promotions of the Direct recruit Assistants and their seniority in their respective positions as on date, shall not be disturbed and the benefit extended to the graduate promotee Assistants by placing them on par with Direct recruit Assistants was to be given effect to prospectively.

♡♡♡

NINE

MADHAVI VS. CHAGAN AND ORS., 2020

Hon'ble Judges/Coram:

L. Nageswara Rao, Hemant Gupta and Ajay Rastogi, JJ.

Equivalent Citation: 2021(6)ABR378, 2021(5)ALLMR820, 2021(1)BLJ167, 2021(1)ESC78(SC), 2020(4)LLN529(SC), 2021 (1) SCJ 173, MANU/SC/0929/2020

Relevant Section/provisions: Section 5(5) of the Maharashtra Employees of Private Schools (Conditions of Service) Regulation Act, 1977

Number of Pages in the Original Judgment: 11

Case Note:

Service - Promotion - Post of 'Head Master' - Seniority - Determination thereof - Section 5(5) of the Maharashtra Employees of Private Schools (Conditions of Service) Regulation Act, 1977 - The Maharashtra Employees of Private Schools (Conditions of Service) Rules, 1981 - Appellant's promotion to post of Head Master challenged - Respondent contended promotion to be illegal as Appellant even employed earlier was not regular - Appellant's seniority was challenged - Whether Appellant was wrongly considered above in seniority over Respondent for promotion?

Brief Facts:

The present dispute was in respect of appointment of Appellant as the Head Master of the School. Respondent claimed that he was appointed on regular basis on 1.8.1985 as against Appellant who was appointed against a temporary vacancy on 16.7.1985. Respondent challenged the appointment contending that he is senior to Appellant and in terms of the Rules, he would be entitled to be promoted as Head Master. School Tribunal dismissed the plea. High Court also dismissed the appeal with the detailed reasoning.

An application for review was then filed and the same was allowed vide impugned judgment.

Held, while allowing the Appeals:

i. High Court failed to appreciate the distinction between Clause 1 and Clause 2 of Schedule 'F' of the Rules. Clause 1 was the subject matter of interpretation by this Court in Viman Vaman Awale and Clause 2 was the subject matter of interpretation in Bhawna. Vaijanath also dealt with promotion to the post of Head Master of a School falling in Clause 1 of Schedule 'F'. Since the School in question is a secondary school, therefore, Clause 2 of Schedule 'F' will determine the seniority. Chagan was not a trained teacher to be part of Category 'C' at the time of his appointment on 1.8.1985 and he was rightly placed in Category 'E' on account of his qualification but he upgraded his qualifications, and hence was placed in Category 'D' and 'C' on acquiring graduation and B.Ed. degrees respectively.

ii. Keeping in view the principle laid down in Vaijanath, Madhavi was qualified for appointment as a temporary teacher as she was a graduate and also possessed B.Ed. degree. Her appointment was thus in accordance with Section 5(5) of the Act, so was the appointment of the other private Respondents. However, Chagan could not be treated to be part of Category 'C' from the date of his initial appointment i.e. 1.8.1985 as he was neither a graduate nor a trained teacher when he was appointed. Also, Chagan was not even a trained teacher on the date of his appointment and thus cannot claim seniority on such ground from the date of his initial appointment.

iii. Thus, the judgment of the High Court in review cannot be sustained in law and the same is hence set aside. The Writ Petition is ordered to be dismissed. The present appeals allowed and the contempt petition also dismissed.

TEN

Manohar Lal Jat and Ors. Vs. The State of Rajasthan and Ors., 2020

Hon'ble Judges/Coram:

Indira Banerjee and S. Ravindra Bhat, JJ.

Equivalent Citation: 2021(1)ESC143(SC), 2021(1)SCT51(SC), 2020(3)SLJ533(SC), 2021(1)SLR89(SC), MANU/SC/0900/2020

Relevant Section/provisions: Rule 27 of the Rajasthan Commercial Taxes Subordinate Services (General Branch) Rules, 1975

Number of Pages in the Original Judgment: 10

Case Note:

Service - Seniority - Claim thereupon - Determination thereof - Rule 27 of the Rajasthan Commercial Taxes Subordinate Services (General Branch) Rules, 1975 - Claims respectively raised between direct recruit departmental promotes - Effect of Amendment in Rule relevant in the year 2002 - Whether claim of direct recruit to prevail over departmental promotes or otherwise?

Brief Facts:

The present appeals challenged impugned finding given by High Court's Division Bench that set aside an order made by the learned single judge holding that the present Appellants (direct recruit/ DRs) were not entitled to claim seniority over and above the Respondents, hereafter called departmental promotes or DPs). The DRs had approached the High Court in the first instance, claiming that the seniority list, showing the DPs in earlier positions, was untenable; the single judge allowed that petition. The Division Bench has, however, allowed the Appellants to question the eligibility of DPs to be recruited.

Held, while dismissing the Appeals:

i. On a plain reading of the entire Rule (Rule 27 [1] and the two provisos) what is evident is that (a) before the amendment of 2002, seniority of personnel appointed to the "lowest categories of posts" in any department was to be determined as from the date of appointment; however, for promotees, it was to be from the date of selection; (b) after the amendment of 2002, seniority has to be fixed (by reason of Rule 27(1)) as on the date of appointment to the post or service; (c) however, in the case of pre-state integration of state (of Rajasthan) or pre-integration of services, seniority could be "modified or altered by the Appointing Authority on an ad hoc basis"- this clearly was meant to be a "sunset" clause, i.e. operative for a limited period; (d) the second proviso,-which is the one pressed into service by the DRs, states that seniority of those selected earlier will be determined over those selected latter.
ii. Plainly, the principal mandate of the Rule is that seniority is determined on the basis of date of appointment ("shall be fixed from the date of their appointment").
iii. Keeping in mind that the advertisements (for filling the entire cadre, in both the quotas or streams of recruitment) were issued one after the other, and more importantly, that this was the first selection and recruitment to a newly created cadre, the delay which occurred on account of administrative exigencies (and also the completion of procedure, such as verification of antecedents) the seniority of the promotees given on the basis of their dates of appointment, is justified by Rule 27 in this case. The impugned judgment not erroneous and does not call for interference. Appeals dismissed.

ELEVEN

WARAD MURTI MISHRA VS. STATE OF MADHYA PRADESH AND ORS., 2020

Hon'ble Judges/Coram:

U.U. Lalit and Indu Malhotra, JJ.

Equivalent Citation: 2020(2)ESC512(SC), 2020(2)ESC356(SC), 2020(3)JLJ1, (2020)7SCC509, 2020(3)SCT409(SC), 2020(3)SLJ114(SC)

Relevant Section/provisions: Rule 8 of Rules of 1961, Rule 13 of Rules of 1975

Number of Pages in the Original Judgment: 15

Case Note:

Service - Seniority - Refer to bench - Appellant joined service as Deputy Collector - Appellant was initially put on probation for two years and was required to clear departmental examination within that period - Appellant could, however, clear examination more than three years after initial appointment - While issuing Seniority List, Appellant and similarly situated persons were declared as confirmed/permanent on date when they had cleared the examination, which incidentally was later than date of confirmation of the officers in subsequent selection - In challenge raised by concerned candidates, Division Bench of High Court held that Petitioners could not be awarded seniority below persons who had been selected/appointed under subsequent selection process - Thereafter, matter was referred to Full Bench of High Court - Full Bench held that probationer who had passed departmental examination prescribed either in Rules or in order of appointment at end of extended period of probation shall be deemed to be a confirmed employee and shall be assigned seniority accordingly - State challenged decision of Full Bench which were dismissed by this Court and review petition arising therefrom was dismissed by this Court - Subsequently, Writ Petitions were filed by Appellant and similarly situated persons seeking direction to grant them seniority from initial date of appointment in their respective batches - Division Bench held that Full Bench had only considered Rule 8 of Rules of 1961, although it ought to have considered Rule 13 of Rules of 1975 and if there was any inconsistency, departmental Rules would govern field - Division Bench refer judgment of Full Bench to Larger Bench to answer certain issues - Hence, present appeal - Whether Division Bench erred in referring judgment of Full Bench pertaining to seniority to Larger Bench was sustainable.

Brief Facts:

The Appellant joined the service as Deputy Collector after being selected by the Public Service Commission. The Appellant was initially put on probation for two years and was required to clear a departmental examination within that period. In terms of the concerned Rules, the probation period can be extended for one year but the departmental examination must be cleared during the extended period. The Appellant could, however, clear the examination more than three years after the initial appointment. While issuing the Seniority List, the Appellant and similarly situated persons were declared as confirmed/permanent on the date when they had cleared the examination, which incidentally was later than the date of confirmation of the officers in the subsequent selection. In a challenge raised by the concerned candidates, the Division Bench of the High Court held that Petitioners could not be awarded seniority below the persons who had been selected/appointed under the subsequent selection process. The division bench once Public Service Commission or the appointing authority undertakes the process for selection then for that class this was the end of matter. After such selection the persons would be appointed on probation or permanently. In case persons are appointed on probation then they would be required to complete the period of probation successfully and on completion of the period they would not be reappointed or reselected but they would be confirmed on the post. Thereafter, the matter was referred to the Full Bench of the High Court. The full bench held that a probationer who had passed the departmental examination prescribed either in he Rules or in the order of appointment at the end of extended period of probation shall be deemed to be a confirmed employee and shall be assigned seniority accordingly. It was held that a probationer who had not been able to pass the departmental examination prescribed either in the Rules or in the order of appointment at the end of extended period of probation shall be deemed to be temporary employee under Rule 8 (7) of the 1961 Rules. State challenged the decision of the Full Bench by filing Special Leave Petition which were dismissed by this Court. Review Petition arising therefrom was dismissed by this Court. Subsequently, Writ Petitions were filed by the Appellant and similarly situated persons seeking direction to grant them seniority from the initial date of appointment in their respective batches in view of the provisions contained in Rule 12 (1)(a) and (f) of 1961 Rules, though they had not passed the departmental examination either within the initial period of probation of two years or within the extended period of probation of one year. The Division Bench considered the decision of the Full Bench and observed that Sub-rule (7) of Rule 8 ibid indicates that if a probationer had not been confirmed under Sub-rule (6) nor discharged under Sub-rule (4) then he would be deemed to be a temporary government servant but Rules of 1975 makes it clear that in case either in Sub-rule (4) or in Sub-rule (5) if confirmation order had not been issued, in both the cases he would be deemed to be the temporary government servant and his service conditions shall be governed by Rules of 1960. The Full Bench had only considered the Rule 8 of the Rules of 1961, although it ought to have considered Rule 13 of the Rules of 1975 and if there is any inconsistency, the departmental Rules would govern the field as per Rule 3 of the Rules of 1961 as well of the Rules of 1975. The division bench refer the judgment of the Full Bench to the Larger Bench to answer the certain issues.

Held, while disposing off the appeal:

i. It was true that the decisions of the Division Bench and the Full Bench were challenged and not only the Special Leave Petitions but the Review Petitions were also dismissed. But as observed by the Division Bench in the instant case, the effect of Rule 13 of 1975 Rules was not considered on the earlier occasions. Since the Division Bench had now made a reference to a larger bench, this court did not propose to enter into the matter and decide the controversy but leave it to the High Court to consider and decide all the issues.

ii. Whether the reference was justified or not will certainly be considered by the bench answering the reference. However, direct that the matters shall first be placed before a bench of three Judges, which may consider whether the decision of the Full Bench on the earlier occasion requires reconsideration. The bench may consider the effect of non-consideration of Rule 13 of 1975 Rules on the earlier occasion as well as the impact of the decisions of this Court on the controversy in question. The matters shall be considered purely on merits and without being influenced by the dismissal of Special Leave Petitions by this Court on the earlier occasions or dismissal of the Review Petitions.

ppp

TWELVE

Pravakar Mallick and Ors. Vs. The State of Orissa and Ors., 2020

Hon'ble Judges/Coram:

Mohan M. Shantanagoudar and R. Subhash Reddy, JJ.

Equivalent Citation: AIR2020SC2122, 2021(3)BLJ471, 2020(4)CGLJ289, 2020(I)CLR(SC)989, 2020(1)ESC233(SC), 2020(2)J.L.J.R.383, 2020(2)KLJ498, 2020(I)OLR625, 2020(3)PLJR46, (2020)15SCC297, 2020 (7-8) SCJ 296, 2020(3)SLJ107(SC), 2020(3)SLR278(SC), MANU/SC/0379/2020

Relevant Section/provisions: Article 16(4A) of Constitution of India

Number of Pages in the Original Judgment: 07

Case Note:

Service - Seniority on promotion - Quashing of resolution - State Government had issued Resolution issuing instructions to all departments of Government to extend benefit of seniority for scheduled caste and scheduled tribe government servants on promotion by virtue of Rule of reservation - Pursuant to such Government Resolution, Gradation List was prepared by altering seniority of Respondent-writ Petitioners - Respondent approached Tribunal but said application was dismissed on ground that it was premature - Thereafter, Respondent had approached High Court for quashment of Government Resolution and consequential Gradation List - Writ petition was allowed by High Court mainly on ground that,

Government Resolution could neither be termed as law in exercise of enabling power of State under Article 16(4A), nor did it satisfy parameters laid down by this Court - High Court quashed Government Resolution and consequential Gradation List - Hence, present appeal - Whether SC/ST candidates were entitled to claim seniority in promoted categories over general category candidates pursuant to resolution issued by State Government.

Brief Facts:

The Respondent-writ Petitioners were appointed to Orissa Administrative Service-II (OAS-II) posts pursuant to selections made by the Public Service Commission. They were assigned different ranks in the merit list for their respective batches prepared by the Public Service Commission. In the said merit list, persons belonging to SC/ST category, who were appointed against the reserved vacancies were placed below the writ Petitioners. The State Government had issued a resolution for fixation of seniority of Scheduled Caste/Scheduled Tribe (SC/ST) government servants on promotion by virtue of Rule of reservation, the State Government had issued instructions to the effect that the Catch Up Principle adopted earlier by the State Government in General Administration Department Resolution shall not be followed any longer. It was further ordered that the government servants belonging to SCs/STs shall retain their seniority in the case of promotion by virtue of Rule of reservation. In the said G.O. it was further clarified that the government servants belonging to general/OBC category promoted later would be placed junior to the SC/ST government servants promoted earlier, by virtue of Rule of reservation. The High Court had allowed the abovementioned writ petition and the connected writ petitions and quashed the resolution and Gradation List mainly on the ground that, unless and until the State Government makes a law for conferring the benefit of promotion with consequential seniority to SC/ST candidates, they were not entitled to claim seniority in the promoted categories over the general category candidates.

Held, while dismissing the appeal:

i. After Constitution (Eighty-Fifth) Amendment Act, 2001, amending Article 16(4A) of the Constitution which enabled the State to extend the benefit of promotion with consequential seniority by examining the adequacy of representation to scheduled castes and scheduled tribes in the State services, the State had not made any provision, either by way of legislation or by an executive order, to extend such benefit in the Class-I Services. The State specifically admitted that the Govt. had not issued any executive order or had passed any legislation. The Government Resolution was issued merely based on the instructions issued by the Government of India, without examining the adequacy of representation in posts. As was evident from the order of the High Court, the State in its counter affidavit had taken the stand that there was no necessity for bringing out any law to extend the benefit of seniority for those who were promoted in reserved vacancies. Government Resolution could neither be termed as law made in exercise of enabling power of the State under Article 16(4A), nor does it satisfy the parameters laid down in the various decisions of this Court. The Resolution had no legal basis. The Seniority/Gradation List of OAS-I (JB) was prepared correctly by following the ratio laid down by this Court and in absence of any law or decision by way of executive order based on acceptable material for conferring additional benefit of consequential seniority, the Gradation List was prepared by altering the positions which were maintained in the List. While it was open for the State to confer benefit even through an executive order by applying mandatory requirements as contemplated under Article 16(4A) but the Resolution was merely issued by referring to the instructions of the Union of India without examining the adequacy of representation in promotional posts, as held by this Court.

ii. Further, the submission that the benefit of reservation in promotion is given in the services of OAS-I for scheduled caste and scheduled tribe officers as per Section 10 of Orissa Act 38 of 1975, but same could not be countenanced for the reason that such Act was enacted by the State of Orissa in the year 1975 but no provision was brought in such Act for giving the benefit of seniority for the promotees who were promoted in reserved vacancies. In absence of any provision in the said Act for conferring the benefit of seniority, and in absence of any amendment after Constitution (Eighty-Fifth) Amendment Act of 2001, by which Article 16(4A) was amended, benefit of seniority cannot be extended relying on Section 10 of the Act. In view of the stand of the Respondent-State in the counter affidavit filed in the writ petition and further in view of the submission made by the State that no benefit of seniority was extended by any State Act or by any executive order by examining adequate representation in terms of Article 16(4A) of the Constitution, there was no merit in this appeal so as to interfere with the well reasoned judgment of the High Court.

THIRTEEN

C. Jayachandran Vs. State of Kerala and Ors., 2020

Hon'ble Judges/Coram:

U.U. Lalit and Hemant Gupta, JJ.

Equivalent Citation: AIR2020SC3846, ILR2020(1)Kerala928, 2020 (2) KHC 478, 2020(2)KLJ264, 2020(2)KLT402, 2020LabIC3525, (2020)5SCC230, (2020)2SCC(LS)37, 2020 (4) SCJ 612, 2020(2)SCT351(SC), 2020(2)SLJ109(SC), 2020(5)SLR591(SC)

Relevant Section/provisions: Kerala State Higher Judicial Services Special Rules, 1961

Number of Pages in the Original Judgment: 15

Case Note:

Service - Notional seniority - Entitled to - Advertisement was published to fill up posts in Kerala Higher Judicial Service -Appellant was appointed in cadre of District Judge - After advertisement was published for direct recruitment, six officers were promoted by transfer to cadre of District Judge but without prejudice to claim of candidates to be recruited directly from Bar - Appellant submitted representation claiming notional seniority with effect from date of appointment of other candidates through same selection - Administrative Committee found that candidates appointed in excess of quota were entitled to seniority from date such candidates were adjusted against available vacancies within their quota - Consequent to order of Administrative Committee, High Court issued Office Memorandum assigning seniority to Appellant - Such decision of High Court was challenged through Writ Petitions before High Court - Writ petitions were dismissed by Single Bench of High Court - Aggrieved, appeals were preferred before Division Bench of High Court which came to be allowed - High Court found that direct recruits of selection in question were appointed against quota of permanent posts - Division Bench further held that Administrative Committee erred insofar as there was no quota prescribed for by-transfer appointees - Hence, present appeal - Whether Appellant entitled for notional seniority.

Brief Facts:

An advertisement was published to fill up posts in the Kerala Higher Judicial Service in terms of Kerala State Higher Judicial Services Special Rules, 1961. The selection process in pursuance of such advertisement was challenged by the Appellant in respect of minimum age which was fixed as thirty five years. The High Court struck down the eligibility in respect of minimum age. The Special Leave Petition against the said order was dismissed. After the said order, four candidates, were selected against general merit vacancies whereas three others were selected against the posts meant for reserved category. The Appellant disputed such selection process before this Court. Writ Petition filed by the Appellant was disposed of by this Court on 14th May, 2010 granting liberty to the Appellant to move the High Court after observing that the writ petition involves an important question of public importance. It is thereafter, the Appellant filed Writ Petition before the High Court challenging the grant of moderation/grace marks to the candidates who were appointed and sought his appointment as District and Sessions Judge. The said writ petition was allowed by the Division Bench of the High Court. The grant of moderation marks was found to be unsustainable. The High Court directed to recast the select list. In pursuance of the said select list, the Appellant was appointed in the cadre of District Judge. After the advertisement was published for direct recruitment, six officers were promoted by transfer to the cadre of District Judge but without prejudice to the claim of the candidates to be recruited directly from Bar. The Appellant submitted a representation claiming notional seniority with effect from the date of appointment of other candidates through the same selection, as directed by the High Court. The High Court issued notice to the Officers appointed by transfer to consider the representation filed by four direct recruits claiming seniority over District Judges appointed by transfer from amongst Sub-Judges/Chief Judicial Magistrates. The Administrative Committee found that the candidates appointed in excess of the quota were entitled to seniority from the date the such candidates were adjusted against the available vacancies within their quota. Consequent to the order of the Administrative Committee, the High Court issued an Office Memorandum assigning seniority to the Appellant and other persons. Such decision of the High Court was challenged. All the writ petitions were dismissed by the Single Bench of the High Court. Aggrieved against the order passed by the Single Bench of the High Court, three intra-court appeals were preferred before the Division Bench of the High Court which came to be allowed. The High Court found that direct recruits of the selection in question were appointed against the quota of the permanent posts. The Division Bench of the High Court further held that the Administrative Committee erred insofar as there is no quota prescribed for by-transfer appointees. The quota was only for direct recruits and confined to permanent posts in the cadre of District Judges. There was no reversion that has been affected to accommodate the direct recruits. The High Court further held that the Administrative Committee did not have the power to decide on the seniority dispute between by-transfer appointees and direct recruits.

Held, while allowing the appeal:

i. The Division Bench of the High Court had directed to re-cast the seniority amongst the seven shortlisted candidates. The Appellant was one of them. The challenge to the said order by three affected candidates remained unsuccessful when SLP was dismissed by this Court. The SLP was filed by the candidates who were granted benefit of moderation of marks. Once the direction of the Division Bench had attained finality, the Appellant was entitled to seniority as per the select list to be revised as per merit of the candidates. In terms of Rule 6(2), the seniority is to be determined by the serial order in which the name appeared in the appointment order. The argument of Respondent No. 5 that the Appellant was not appointed by the same appointment order, therefore, the Appellant could not claim seniority was not tenable. The Appellant was entitled to be appointed along with other three candidates but because of the action of the High Court in adopting moderation of marks, the Appellant was excluded from appointment. The exclusion of Appellant from appointment was on account of an illegal act by the High Court which had been so found by the judgment. Since the select list had to be revised, the Appellant would be deemed to be the part of the appointment along with other candidates in the same select list. As the actual date of appointment, the Appellant could not actually be treated to be appointed but was entitled to notional appointment from that date and consequential seniority.

ii. The Office Memorandum of Government and later notification of the State Government appointing the Appellant was that of setting aside of selection of three candidates and appointing the Appellant. It was in tune with the merit while preparing the select list. Therefore, such merit could not be disturbed only for the reason that the Appellant had not disputed it for one year and two months after his appointment. Admittedly, a seniority list was circulated before the appointment of the Appellant, thereafter, no seniority list was circulated. The Appellant had already submitted representation claiming seniority which representation was accepted. An employee had no control over the employer to decide the representation or to finalise the seniority as per his wish. The High Court has taken long time to decide the seniority claim. That fact would not disentitle the Appellant to claim seniority from the date the other candidates in the same selection process were appointed. The fact that some of the officers had been given selection grade would not debar the Appellant to claim notional date of appointment as the Appellant had asserted his right successfully before the Division Bench in an earlier round and reiterated such right by way of a representation. The delay in deciding the representation by the High Court could not defeat the rights of the Appellant to claim seniority from the date the other candidates selected in pursuance of the same selection process.

iii. The Division Bench of the High Court had completely erred in law in holding that the Appellant had delayed the challenge of his appointment. The Appellant was appointed pursuant to a direction issued earlier by the Division Bench. The Division Bench had directed to re-cast the select list and in such select list, the name of the Appellant appears at serial number three and that of other candidate at serial number four. The Appellant had submitted the representation within one year and two months of his joining and submitted reminder. It was the High Court which has taken time to take a final call on the representation of the Appellant and other direct recruits. The Appellant was prosecuting his grievances in a legitimate manner of redressal of grievances. Therefore, it could not be said that the claim of the Appellant was delayed as he had not claimed the date of appointment. The Appellant having been factually appointed, he could not assume or claim to assume charge prior to such offer of appointment. The Appellant had to be granted notional seniority from the date the other candidates were appointed in pursuance of the same select list prepared on the basis of the common appointment process.

iv. The argument that grant of selection grade to Respondent Nos. 11 and 12 was earlier in point of time than the Appellant would not confer any better, legal or equitable right. There was specific condition in the letter of appointment by transfer of Respondent Nos. 9-10 that their appointment was without prejudice to the recruitment of direct recruits. Since the rights of the direct recruits were specifically mentioned, such Respondents could not claim any protection of their transfer in the cadre only for the reason that they were granted selection cadre earlier. The finding recorded by the High Court administratively and by the Single Judge was that the appointment of such candidates was beyond their quota meant for appointment by transfer. Therefore, they could not claim any legal or equitable right. Similarly, Respondent Nos. 11-12 were appointed by transfer to the cadre subject to the condition of rights of the candidates in the writ petitions pending at that time. The said writ petitions were decided in the light of the order passed in the earlier writ petition filed by the Appellant. The rights of the Appellant to claim notional seniority thus could not be said to be unjust which was wrongly interfered with by the Division Bench in an intra-Court appeal.

FOURTEEN

PARMESHWAR NANDA AND ORS. VS. THE STATE OF JHARKHAND AND ORS., 2020

Hon'ble Judges/Coram:

L. Nageswara Rao and Hemant Gupta, JJ.

Equivalent Citation: 2020(4)ESC971(SC), [2020(166)FLR885], 2020(1)J.L.J.R.437, 2020(1)PLJR481, (2020)12SCC131, 2020 (6) SCJ 253, 2020(1)SCT817(SC), 2020(3)SLR405(SC), MANU/SC/0138/2020

Relevant Section/provisions: Rules 58 and 59 (1) of Bihar Pension Rules, 1950

Number of Pages in the Original Judgment: 09

Case Note:

Service - Pensionary benefits - Counting of period - Rules 58 and 59 (1) of Bihar Pension Rules, 1950 - Some Appellants were appointed as Adult Education Supervisors and some were appointed in ministerial cadre such as Stenographer, Clerk cum Accountant, Clerk cum Typist, Peon as well as Drivers - Government issued notification for absorption of employees - As per notification, surplus employees absorbed were to be treated as new appointments and services rendered by them prior to their declaration as surplus would not be counted for purpose of their seniority and pay protection - Writ petitions came to be filed claiming pensionary benefits and seniority before High Court - High Court held that services rendered by Appellants under Adult Education and Non-Formal Education Project could not be counted under Government scheme for purpose of pensionary benefits after Appellants were appointed by State - Hence, present appeal - Whether services rendered by Appellants under Adult Education and Non-Formal Education Project could be counted for purpose of pensionary benefits.

Brief Facts:

The some Appellants were appointed as Adult Education Supervisors and some were appointed in ministerial cadre such as Stenographer, Clerk cum Accountant, Clerk cum Typist, Peon as well as Drivers. The Government issued a notification for absorption of the employees engaged in the Project in the Departments of Food, Public Distribution and Consumer Affairs, Finance, Social Welfare, Women and Child Development, Urban Development etc. on different posts, in their respective prescribed scales of pay. As per the notification, the surplus employees absorbed were to be treated as new appointments and the services rendered by them prior to their declaration as surplus would not be counted for the purpose of their seniority and pay protection. The writ petitions came to be filed claiming pensionary benefits and seniority before the High Court. It was the stand of the writ Petitioners that they are being treated as fresh appointees and their past service has not been counted for the purposes of seniority or fixation of their initial salary. The High Court had held that the services rendered by the Appellants under the Adult Education and Non-Formal Education Project could not be counted under a Government scheme for the purpose of pensionary benefits after the Appellants were appointed by the State.

Held, while dismissing the appeals:

i. The Appellants were appointed under a specific Scheme i.e. the Project. Such project was not a permanent establishment of the Government as it was meant for a specific purpose funded by the Central Government for a specified period. The appointment of the Appellants under the Project was not a part of any cadre of the State Government. Therefore, the first condition of Rule 58 that the service rendered must be under the State Government was not satisfied by the Appellants having been appointed under the Project. The second condition that employment must be substantive and permanent was again not satisfied by the Appellants as the employment of the Appellants was under the Project. A permanent post in terms of Rule 31 of the Rules means a post carrying a definite rate of pay and that was sanctioned without a time limit. The appointment of the Appellants under the project was not in a pay scale nor was it sanctioned without a time limit. Further, substantive pay was defined in Rule 38 of the Rules as a person who is appointed in a cadre. At best, the Appellants satisfied only the third condition i.e. that they were paid by the Government.

ii. If the first and second conditions mentioned in Rule 58 of the Rules were not satisfied, the State Government could declare any specified kind of service rendered in a non-gazetted capacity to qualify for pension. The Circular deals with pensionary benefits to a temporary Government servant. The Appellants were never appointed by the Government either on a temporary or on permanent basis. The Appellants were engaged under the Project i.e. a scheme, therefore, the benefit of such a Circular could not be claimed by the Appellants. Still further, Sub-rule (1) of Rule 59 of the Rules empowers the State to declare any specific kind of service to qualify for pension. The notification for absorption and the subsequent letter of appointments did not contain any condition that the services rendered by the Appellants under the Project shall qualify for pension. The policy decision contemplates that it was a fresh appointment and no benefit either of seniority or pay protection shall be given. The Appellants had not disputed such condition of appointment having been appointed under such policy decision vide the notification. The Circular had not granted pensionary benefits. In the absence of any specific condition in the Circular to grant pensionary benefits, it was not possible to read that pensionary benefits are to be granted to the erstwhile employees of the Project. The Appellants could not turn around to say that the services rendered by them under the Project shall be counted for pension. The Circular was not even remotely applicable to the employees appointed under the Project as the very nature of the appointment was for a specific purpose and not for an unlimited period of time.

iii. Since the Appellants were absorbed as fresh appointees without pay protection and seniority, as a consequence thereof, they would not be entitled to count their past service rendered under the Project for the purpose of pension. Thus, there was no error in the order passed by the High Court which may warrant interference in the present appeals.

ÞÞÞ

FIFTEEN

BAJRANG LAL SHARMA VS. C.K. MATHEW AND ORS., 2020

Hon'ble Judges/Coram:

U.U. Lalit, Indira Banerjee and M.R. Shah, JJ.

Equivalent Citation: 2020(215)AIC229, 2020 (4) CCC 339 , 2020(2)SCT76(SC), 2020(4)SLR528(SC), MANU/SC/0076/2020

Relevant Section/provisions: Rule 33 of RAS Rules, 1954; Article 16(4-A) of Constitution of India

Number of Pages in the Original Judgment: 16

Case Note:

Contempt of Court - Consequential seniority - Wilful disobedience - Contempt Petitioner had filed writ petition before High Court against notification issued by State providing for consequential seniority and promotion to members of Scheduled Caste and Scheduled Tribe communities - High Court quashed notifications and all consequential actions and certain directions were issued - High Court held that no exercise was undertaken to acquire quantifiable data regarding inadequacy of representation of SC and ST - State Government constituted Committee to look into different aspects relating to reservation in promotion and consequential seniority - In Contempt Petition filed earlier in High Court seeking implementation of directions issued by High Court, High Court found alleged contemnors to be guilty of violation of order passed by High Court - Matter again reached this Court in form of challenge to said decision of High Court - It was thus found by this Court that there was no willful and deliberate violation - Thereafter, instant Contempt Petitions were filed setting out grievance that this court had issued order whereby direction was issued to all departments to publish seniority lists and make promotions on basis of notification and action of State of making promotions on basis of Notification was in blatant contempt to directions given by this Court - Whether State and its authorities were guilty of willful and deliberate violation of order passed by this court in respect of consequential seniority and promotion.

Brief Facts:

The Contempt Petitioner filed writ petition before the High Court for quashing the notification providing for consequential seniority and promotion to the members of the Scheduled Caste and Scheduled Tribe communities. The High Court quashed the notifications and all consequential actions with certain directions. The High Court held that no exercise was undertaken in terms of Article 16(4-A) of the Constitution to acquire quantifiable data regarding inadequacy of the representation of the Scheduled Caste (SC) and Scheduled Tribe (ST) communities in public services, was accepted. The challenge to the judgment of the High Court was considered by this Court and by its decision in Suraj Bhan and the view taken by the High Court was affirmed. In Civil Contempt Petition which was filed earlier in the High Court seeking implementation of the directions issued by the High Court. The High Court by its judgment and order dated 23.02.2012 found the alleged contemnors to be guilty of violation of the judgment and order passed by the High Court. The matter again reached this Court in the form of challenge to said decision of the High Court and was dealt with by this Court in its decision in Salauddin. The issue whether the State and its authorities were guilty of willful and deliberate violation of binding directions was considered by this Court and it was found that there was no willful and deliberate violation, that the State Government had appointed the Bhatnagar Committee to collect the data necessary in terms of the judgment and Order passed by this Court in M. Nagaraj. Thereafter instant Contempt Petitions were filed setting out the grievance that this court had issued a order whereby direction was issued to all the departments to publish the seniority lists and make promotions on the basis of the notification and the action of the State of making promotions on the basis of the Notification was in blatant contempt to the directions given by this Court.

Held, while dismissing the petitions:

i. The law declared by this Court in M. Nagaraj which was followed in Suraj Bhan Meena was clear that in the absence of any quantifiable data relating to the issue of backwardness and inadequacy of representation of the concerned classes in public employment, no benefit of consequential seniority could be extended. Therefore, in Suraj Bhan Meena, the Notifications providing for consequential seniority in promotion to the Members of the SC/ST communities were set aside.

ii. Since the decision in Suraj Bhan Meena was on the premise that no such exercise was undertaken to acquire quantifiable data, the State Government constituted the Bhatnagar Committee. The Committee went into the issues and made certain recommendations based on which a Notification was issued by the State Government. Whether that amounted to contempt or not was a subject matter of discussion before the High Court which, by its judgment and order found said Notification to be not in compliance of binding directions and to be invalid. The challenge in Salauddin was inter alia to the finding arrived at by the High Court in its contempt jurisdiction and the submission advanced by the Attorney General was that in the absence of any substantive writ petition challenging the same, said Notification could not have been questioned in contempt jurisdiction. The decision in Salauddin set aside the view taken by the High Court. Thus, the issuance of Notification was not found to be in contempt nor was it invalidated for being non-compliant of any binding directions.

iii. As a matter of fact, the directions issued by this Court were clear that the State and its authorities were to act in terms of the report of the Bhatnagar Committee in accordance with the decisions in M. Nagaraj and Suraj Bhan Meena. The basic foundation of the present contempt petitions projecting the issuance of Notification to be in contempt of the directions issued by this Court, thus, did not survive. In any case, challenge to said Notification and the report of the Bhatnagar Committee was still pending consideration before the High Court where the correctness and validity thereof would be gone into in accordance with law.

iv. With the decision of this Court in Jarnail Singh, the matter also stands on a slightly modified footing. As concluded by this Court in Jarnail Singh the conclusion in M. Nagaraj that the State had to collect quantifiable data showing backwardness of SC/ST, being contrary to the decision in Indra Sawhney, was held to be invalid. The challenge to the recommendations given by the Bhatnagar Committee and the quantifiable data adverted to by the Committee would therefore had to be seen by the High Court in the light of the directions issued by this Court in Jarnail Singh.

v. It was, thus, clear that all these issues need to be gone into in a substantive challenge and would be beyond the scope of contempt jurisdiction. The issuance of Notification was in exercise of powers vested in the concerned authorities and if the approach and the exercise was otherwise incorrect or wrong, the same could be tested and considered while dealing with the substantive challenge but such issuance could not be said to be contumacious to invite any action in contempt jurisdiction.

SIXTEEN

THE STATE OF UTTAR PRADESH AND ORS. VS. ALI HUSSAIN ANSARI AND ORS., 2020

Hon'ble Judges/Coram:

S. Abdul Nazeer and Sanjiv Khanna, JJ.

Equivalent Citation: 2020 5 AWC4357SC, 2020(1)ESC82(SC), [2020(166)FLR894], (2020)3SCC99, (2020)1SCC(LS)445, 2020 (5) SCJ 652, 2020(1)SCT719(SC), 2020(1)SLJ423(SC), 2020(3)SLR908(SC), MANU/SC/0036/2020

Relevant Section/provisions: Uttar Pradesh Secondary Services Commission (Removal of Difficulties) Order, 1981

Number of Pages in the Original Judgment: 03

Case Note:

Service - Post-retirement benefit - Legality - State of Uttar Pradesh and its functionaries have filed the present appeal challenging the judgment passed by the High Court, whereby Division Bench had dismissed their appeal and affirmed order passed by learned Single Judge directing grant of consequential benefits in form of post-retirement benefits with seniority in service and promotion(s), but not actual payment of salary for the period between 8th June, 1987 to 30th June, 2006 - Whether directions regarding post-retirement benefit etc. as granted required a modification.

Brief Facts:

Ali Hussain Ansari, the first Respondent, was recommended for appointment as Assistant Teacher in Satya Prakash Vivekanand Inter College, Musahari, Deoria, Uttar Pradesh on ad hoc basis. However, the Committee of Management in the said college, the second Respondent, did not agree and consequently did not issue an appointment letter. They issued an advertisement dated 08.07.1987 for direct recruitment to the post. The names registered with the Employment Exchange were to be included. One Shesh Mani Shukla, upon selection, was appointed and a letter dated 11.09.1987 was written to the District Inspector of Schools, Deoria for approval. However, the District Inspector of Schools, Deoria declined and did not grant approval vide his letter dated 10.12.1987 stating that the selection of Shesh Mani Shukla was contrary to the provisions of Uttar Pradesh Secondary Services Commission (Removal of Difficulties) Order, 1981. By order, the District Inspector of Schools, Deoria refused to grant financial approval for appointment of Shesh Mani Shukla. Aggrieved with the stand taken by the District Inspector of Schools, Deoria, Shesh Mani Shukla assailed these orders in Writ Petition before the High Court. By the interim order, the Appellants before present, including District Inspector of Schools, Deoria and the second Respondent were directed to pay salary to Shesh Mani Shukla. Therefore, and in terms of the interim directions, Shesh Mani Shukla had worked and was paid salary till 23.04.2004, when the High Court was pleased to dismiss the Writ Petition filed by him. Aggrieved, Shesh Mani Shukla had preferred Special Appeal which was dismissed by the Division Bench of the High Court. The appeal against this judgment was also dismissed by this Court vide judgment.

Held, while disposing of the appeal:

i. The first Respondent was issued appointment letter and was appointed as Assistant Professor on 30.06.2006 after the competent authority, that is, the District Inspector of Schools, Deoria had issued order dated 31.07.2006. The first Respondent retired from service on 30.06.2009 on attaining the age of superannuation.
ii. On or about 01.05.2008, the first Respondent had filed Writ Petition before the High Court seeking payment of arrears of salary from 08.06.1987 till 30.06.2006. This Writ Petition was disposed of by order of the learned Single Judge with a direction to the District Inspector of Schools, Deoria to consider and decide the representation made by the first Respondent. The District Inspector of Schools, Deoria vide order

rejected the representation for payment of arrears of salary on the principle of "no work no pay". Aggrieved, the first Respondent had preferred Writ Petition which was disposed of vide judgment directing that the first Respondent would be entitled to consequential benefits including pension benefits with effect from 08.06.1987.

iii. It is apparent that Shesh Mani Shukla upon selection and appointment had filed a Writ Petition in 1988 and worked as an Assistant Professor till 2004. This was in view of the interim directions issued by the High Court. The salary was also paid to Shesh Mani Shukla as the Assistant Professor. The first Respondent though recommended for the vacant post of Assistant Teacher was never issued an appointment letter and was not appointed and had not worked till he joined the post on 30.06.2006. After working for three years, he retired on 30.06.2009. Keeping in view the aforesaid peculiar factual position, present Court would modify the directions given by the Court on the payment of retirement benefits with a direction that the first Respondent would be paid an amount of Rs. 4,00,000 as compensation. This compensation would be in addition to any other benefits which would be payable to the first Respondent in accordance with law treating his date of appointment as 30.06.2006. The appeal is accordingly disposed of.

SEVENTEEN

Dinesh Kumar Gupta and Ors. Vs. High Court of Judicature of Rajasthan and Ors., 2020

Hon'ble Judges/Coram:

U.U. Lalit and Vineet Saran, JJ.

Equivalent Citation: AIR2020SC2270, 2020(3)ALT250, 2020(1)ESC159(SC), 2020 (7-8) SCJ 595, 2020(3)SCT420(SC), 2021(1)SLR726(SC), MANU/SC/0422/2020

Relevant sections: 31(2) and 47(4) of Rajasthan Judicial Service Rules, 2010

Number of pages in original Judgment: 42

Case Note:

Service - Seniority - Allocation of - Rules 31(2) and 47(4) of Rajasthan Judicial Service Rules, 2010 - Present petitions filed for directions that after promulgation of Rajasthan Judicial Service Rules, 2010, all appointments ought to be in conformity with 2010 Rules and allocation of seniority must be in accordance with Cyclic Order provided in Schedule VII to 2010 Rules - Petitions also challenging Provisional Seniority List with regard to cadre of District Judges in Higher Judicial Service in State, on ground that appointments made after 2010 Rules had come into effect, ought to be in accordance with Cyclic Order - Further, Petitioners also seeking benefit of ad-hoc/officiating service put in by Promotees who were promoted on ad-hoc basis as Fast Track Court Judges and also prays for re-determination of vacancies of Direct Recruits submitting that the vacancies earmarked for Direct Recruits were in excess of their quota - Whether judicial officers promoted on ad-hoc basis as Additional District and Sessions were entitled to seniority from date of ad-hoc promotion and Judicial Officers could be placed en-bloc senior to candidates selected in selection process and inter se placement of candidates selected through LCE must be based on merit.

Brief Facts:

A Notification was issued by the High Court determining cumulative vacancies in the cadre of District Judge. Pursuant to the selection undertaken thereafter by Order candidates were appointed to the cadre of District Judge, which included recruitment through Promotion, LCE and Direct Recruitment. The Petitioners were promoted to the cadre of District Judge. Thereafter, a Provisional Seniority List was issued. The names of all the concerned candidates were mentioned in the Provisional Seniority List. The candidates, who were successful in LCE were given the original order of Seniority in the feeder cadre without giving them any benefit for having successfully cleared the LCE. Further the Judicial Officers promoted were en-bloc placed above all the appointees pursuant to selection. The petitions were filed in this court submitting inter alia that post the coming into effect of 2010 Rules, all the appointments in the categories of selection through LCE and Direct Recruitment had to be in conformity with 2010 Rules and in tune with the Cyclic Order and placement of the Judicial Officers whose Appointment Orders were issued after the process was undertaken for selection of candidates through LCE and Direct Recruitment, was not correct.

Held, while disposing off the petitions:

i. The decisions in Debabrata Dash and V. Venkata Prasad were in the context where serving Judicial Officers were granted ad-hoc promotions as Fast Track Court Judges, while in C. Yamini the members of the Bar were appointed as Fast Track Court Judges and these decisions thus completely conclude the issue. As had been held in said decisions, the reckonable date has to be the date when substantive appointment is made and not from the date of the initial ad-hoc appointment or promotion.

ii. It was relevant to note that the Notification had invited application for filling up vacancies by Direct Recruitments and vacancies by Promotion through LCE. This was preceded by determination of vacancies through Notification. After the process initiated in terms of said Notification was cancelled, a fresh determination of the vacancies was undertaken and the Notification now found vacancies for Direct Recruitments, for Promotion through LCE and for Regular Promotion. Thus, the vacancies which became available post the Notification were also taken into account. The Report shows that some of the selected candidates in the process pursuant to the Notification had not even participated in the earlier process of 2010. In the premises, if the submission that the process initiated under the Notification must be held to be in continuation of the earlier selection of 2010 was accepted, it would amount to conferring undue advantages upon persons who either had not participated in the process of 2010 or who were not even eligible in 2010. The Report therefore, correctly appreciated the fact situation on record and concluded that it would not be in continuation of the earlier process.

iii. The candidates selected through LCE and Direct Recruitment could not claim to be clubbed with the Judicial Officers promoted in substantive capacity and could not claim appropriate placement in accordance with the Cyclic Order. Thus, the Judicial Officers were rightly placed en-bloc senior to all the candidates selected through the process initiated pursuant to the Notification.

iv. It was relevant to notice the emphasis placed by this Court in All India Judges Association while directing that twenty five per cent of the posts in the cadre of the District Judge be filled through LCE. It was stated that there should be an incentive amongst relatively junior and other officers to improve and to compete with each other so as to excel and get accelerated promotion. The relevant direction again stressed that twenty five per cent quota for promotion through LCE be strictly on the basis of merit. Rule 31(2) of 2010 Rules also uses the expression strictly on the basis of merit while dealing with posts to be filled in through LCE. The merit was to be assessed in terms of the scheme laid down in the relevant Schedule. After considering various parameters stated in said Schedule, the successful candidates were selected on the basis of merit. The list of successful candidates becomes the basis for final selection subject to qualifying parameters such as suitability, medical fitness etc. However, placing reliance on Rule 47(4), the Committee in its Report held that the *inter se* seniority of persons promoted to the District Judge Cadre in the same year ought to be the same as it was in the posts held by them at the time of promotion. If the list was to be drawn up according to merit, it is possible that the last person in the list of selectees may be the senior most and going by the Report of the Committee, if all the selectees are promoted in the same year such last person may as well be at the top of the list of promotees through LCE. In that event, the seniority shall become the governing criteria and the excellence on part of a comparatively junior candidate may recede in the background. Instead of giving incentive to comparatively junior and other officers, the entire examination process would stand reduced to a mere qualifying examination rather than a competitive examination affording opportunity to meritorious candidates. The criteria shall then become seniority subject to passing the LCE. The direction issued in All India Judges Association to afford an incentive to meritorious candidates regardless of their seniority would not thus be carried out. The general principle appearing in Rule 47(4) must, therefore, give way to the special dispensation in Rule 31(2) of 2010 Rules. The High Court in its Report completely failed to appreciate the true character of LCE and reservation of certain quota for that category. Thus, the inter se placement of the candidates selected through LCE must be based on merit and not on the basis of the seniority in the erstwhile cadre.

v. The Petitioners came to be appointed on ad-hoc basis to man the Fast Track Courts after 2010 Rules came into effect. Even if their services were continued after abolition of Fast Track Courts, that by itself would not confer any right on them. They came to be substantively promoted to the Cadre of District Judge. Their entitlement on substantive basis had to be reckoned only from the date of appointment to District judge and not from any earlier date. Thus, the Report of the High Court did not call for any modification.

ppp

EIGHTEEN

NAND KUMAR MANJHI AND ORS. VS. THE STATE OF BIHAR AND ORS., 2019

Hon'ble Judges/Coram:

U.U. Lalit and Indu Malhotra, JJ.

Equivalent Citation: AIR2019SC2204, 2019(3)BLJ240, 2019(2)ESC305(SC), 2019(3)J.L.J.R.34, 2019LabIC2586, 2019(3)PLJR34, 2019(6)SCALE614, (2019)14SCC67, (2020)1SCC(LS)774, 2019(2)SCT742(SC), 2019(2)SLJ1(SC), 2019(6)SLR151(SC), MANU/SC/0590/2019

Relevant sections: Rule35 of the Bihar Forest Service Rules, 1953

Number of pages in original Judgment: 10

Case Note:

Service - Seniority list - Validity of - Provisional Seniority List was published, wherein Appellants were placed below Direct Recruits and Promotees - Objections were raised by Appellants regarding their placement in Seniority List but same was rejected by High-Level Scrutiny Committee - Final Seniority List was published and Appellants were placed at bottom of Seniority List - Writ petition filed before High Court, whereby Single judge held that Appellants were rightly placed at bottom of the Seniority List - Appellants preferred Letters Patent Appeal before Division Bench which was also dismissed - Hence, present appeal - Whether impugned seniority list placed Appellants at bottom was sustainable.

Brief Facts:

Provisional Seniority List was published, wherein the Appellants were placed below the Direct Recruits and Promotees. Objections were raised by the Appellants which were rejected by the High-Level Scrutiny Committee. The Final Seniority List was published on 02.07.2010. The Appellants were placed at the bottom of the Seniority List. The writ petition filed before the High Court whereby held that the Appellants were rightly placed at the bottom of the Seniority List. Appellants preferred Letters Patent Appeal before a Division Bench which was dismissed by holding that the Appellants could not claim seniority on the principle of continuous officiation from the date of their appointment.

Held, while dismissing the appeal:

An appointment in substantive capacity was one which was not fortuitous or ad hoc, and was made in compliance with the extant Rules and Regulations. he Appellants had admittedly secured appointment as ACFs through the back-door by making various representations to the Chief Minister, the Minister of Forests and Environment and the Secretary, Department of Forests and Environment. Pursuant to these representations, the State appointed the Appellants purportedly with reference to the advertisement. This was completely illegal and fortuitous, since the posts advertised had been filled up from the merit list. There was no provision for maintaining a Wait List under the Bihar Forest Service Rules, 1953. Hence, the appointment of the Appellants was wholly illegal and contrary to the statutory rules. The High Court rightly held that the seniority of the Appellants could be reckoned only from the date of their regularisation in service, and not from the date of their initial appointment, as claimed by them. The Appellants had secured an illegal appointment through the backdoor, which was wholly illegal and de hors the Statutory Rules.. As per Rule 35 of the Bihar Forest Service Rules, 1953 the seniority of officers shall be determined with reference to the date of their substantive appointment to the service. Hence, the claim for seniority from the date of their initial appointment was wholly untenable, misconceived, and contrary to statutory Rules..

NINETEEN

DHARMENDRA PRASAD AND ORS. VS. SUNIL KUMAR AND ORS., 2019

Hon'ble Judges/Coram:

L. Nageswara Rao and Hemant Gupta, JJ.

Equivalent Citation: 2020(2)LLN31(SC), 2019(17)SCALE564, (2020)2SCC146, (2020)1SCC(LS)263, MANU/SC/1687/2019

Relevant sections: Regulation 23 of Uttar Pradesh Jal Nigam Subordinate Engineering Service Regulations, 1978

Number of pages in original Judgment: 07

Case Note:

Service - Seniority - Fixation of - Regulation 23 of Uttar Pradesh Jal Nigam Subordinate Engineering Service Regulations, 1978 - Advertisement was issued for filling up of posts of Junior Engineer (Civil) - Pursuant to advertisement, selection process was completed and result was declared - Appointment orders were given to candidates - Thereafter, seniority list was published on basis of merit list prepared while declaring result - Said seniority list became subject matter of challenge before Tribunal, which stand dismissed - Said order was made subject matter of challenge before High Court - High Court held that since there was no dispute about dates of appointment of candidates, seniority had to be prepared in terms of Regulation 23 based upon dates of appointment rather than merit - Hence, present appeal - Whether High Court erred in holding that seniority had to be prepared in terms of Regulation 23 based upon dates of appointment rather than merit.

Brief Facts:

An advertisement was issued by the Nigam for filling up of posts of Junior Engineer (Civil). Pursuant to the above said advertisement, the selection process was completed and a merit list on the basis of marks obtained in the written test and interview was published. The result was declared separately for the candidates belonging to different categories i.e. General category, OBC, SC and ST. Thereafter, the appointment orders were given to the candidates in each category proportionate to the quota reserved for the reserved category candidates. Thereafter, a tentative seniority list was published based upon the merit list prepared on the basis of the marks obtained in the written test and interview. Objections were filed to such tentative seniority list. The final seniority list was published on the basis of the merit list prepared while declaring the result. The said seniority list became subject matter of challenge before the Tribunal. The Tribunal dismissed the petition. Thereafter, a review petition was filed which was also dismissed. The said order was made subject matter of challenge before the High Court. The High Court held that since there was no dispute about the dates of appointment of the candidates, the seniority has to be prepared in terms of Regulation 23 based upon dates of appointment rather than merit, as the Rule to determine seniority was from the date of appointment.

Held, while allowing the appeal:

i. The method of giving appointment to the senior most person of each category was only a fortuitous circumstance as such appointments were made dehors the merit. Regulation 20 mandates the appointing authority to make the appointments from amongst the candidates in order in which they stand in the list prepared under Regulations 16(2), 17 or 18. Any appointment made by the Nigam in contravention of the statutory Regulations could not defeat the rights of the Appellants only because they had not challenged the appointment of their juniors at an earlier point of time. Regulation 23 provides that seniority of persons appointed in any branch of service shall be made as per substantive appointment. The appointment in Regulation 23 has to be read in terms of Regulation 20 mandating the manner of appointment. Therefore, irrespective of the date of appointment, the seniority had to be fixed as per the merit of the candidates determined by the Selection Committee.

ii. However, it was found that Regulation 6 itself contemplated that reservation of candidates belonging to SC, ST, Backward Classes and the candidates of other categories shall be in accordance with the orders of the Government in force at the time of recruitment. In terms of such Regulations, the Government order becomes applicable to determine the extent of reservation which includes the method of determining seniority as well. Apart from the statutory Regulation 6, even the approval of the State Government to fill up posts specifically mentions that the reservation shall be made as per the hundred points roster as prescribed in the Circular. Admittedly, the seniority had not been framed keeping in view the roster.
iii. There was no merit in the argument raised by the State that the seniority had to be fixed as per Rule 5 of the Uttarakhand Government Servant Seniority Service Rules, 2002. Such Rules were not adopted to be applicable to the Nigam. The Rules were approved by the Board of the Nigam proposing that the provision shall be made in the proposed service Regulations but the Rules were made applicable. Such was the finding recorded by the High Court which was not disputed by the Appellants or by the writ Petitioners. Such Rules had been framed under the proviso to Article 309 of the Constitution and they were not applicable to a creation under a Statute. These Rules were applicable to government servants in respect of whose recruitment and condition of service Rules may be or have been made by the Government under the proviso to Article 309 of the Constitution. Since the employees of the Nigam were not government servants nor were their service conditions governed by Rules framed under the proviso to Article 309 of the Constitution, therefore, such Rules unless adopted by the Nigam could not be extended to the employees of the Nigam.
iv. Therefore, the order of the High Court and that of the Tribunal were not sustainable in law as the seniority list had not been prepared in accordance with the roster which was required to be mandatorily followed in terms of Regulation 6 as well with the approval of the State Government to fill up posts.

TWENTY

R.K. Barwal and Ors. Vs. State of Himachal Pradesh and Ors., 2017

Hon'ble Judges/Coram:

A.K. Sikri and Ashok Bhushan, JJ.

Equivalent Citation: AIR2018SC403, 2018LabIC1069, (2017)16SCC803, 2018 (8) SCJ 275, 2017(4)SCT402(SC), MANU/SC/1156/2017

Relevant sections: Demobilized Armed Forces Personnel (Reservation of Vacancies in Himachal Pradesh State Non-Technical Services) Rules, 1972

Number of pages in original Judgment: 13

Case Note:

Service - Seniority benefits - Entitlement thereto - Demobilized Armed Forces Personnel (Reservation of Vacancies in Himachal Pradesh State Non-Technical Services) Rules, 1972 - Present appeal filed challenging validity of Demobilized Armed Forces Personnel (Reservation of Vacancies in Himachal Pradesh State Non-Technical Services) Rules, 1972 - Whether such ex-service personnel could be given seniority even when they failed in first attempt in securing civil employment - Whether benefit of service rendered in armed forces could be given even if there was significant time lag between release of such personnel by army and securing civil employment.

Brief Facts:

Present appeal filed challenging the validity of Demobilized Armed Forces Personnel (Reservation of Vacancies in the Himachal Pradesh State Non-Technical Services) Rules, 1972. These 1972 Rules provide for reservation to the Released Indian Armed Forces Personnel in non-technical services in the State. Provision was also made in the 1972 Rules for conferring the benefit of counting approved military service of such Released Armed Forces Personnel for the purpose of fixation of their seniority and pay in civil employment.

Held, while dismissing the appeal:

Those who were joining military service even in peace times were faced with difficult situations of proxy war and have also to deal with insurgency and terrorism. It was also a matter of common knowledge that these military personnel were risking their life while dealing with the difficult situations and, in fact, the casualties and fatalities of the soldiers were on the rise. When they leave the military service, as an ex-serviceman, they not only get the benefit of appointment to the civilian post against the quota earmarked for them, they were also getting the benefit of counting of military service when their pay was fixed on their appointment to the civilian post. However, benefit of counting of military service rendered by these ex-servicemen for the purpose of seniority could not be extended to them. Such a benefit was restricted by present Court only to those who joined armed forces during emergency due to foreign aggression. Present Court, while doing so, categorically and repeatedly held that the call of service to nation during war period was on a totally different footing than joining army when the Country was not facing any such foreign aggression. Persons who were commissioned in armed forces when the nation was faced with foreign aggression and the cry of the time was that persons should join armed forces to defend the integrity and sovereignty of the nation, it was stressed that many persons in such situations were not inclined to join the armed forces and only those with the feeling for the honour of the nation rise to such occasions. Such persons joining armed forces at that time, sacrificing their career, had to be treated as a separate class by extending them the benefit in the matter of seniority as well. However, those who joined the armed forces otherwise, they did so in look out of a career and joined such services of their own volition. They were prepared for the normal risk in service of the armed forces. Therefore, benefit of service rendered in armed forces could not be extended to such a class for the purposes of seniority. These persons joined the service to make their career and on their own volition, exercising it as a matter of choice. Their cases were, therefore, on a different footing altogether. After all, if the benefit of armed force services rendered was extended to each and every ex-serviceman for the purpose of seniority, it may result in far reaching implications. Present Court could not shy away from the normal Rule of fixing the seniority, as enunciated in the cases of Direct Recruitment Class II Engineering Officer's Association as well as Aghore Nath Dev, i.e. the seniority of an officer in service was determined with reference to the date of his entry in the service, which is consistent with the requirement of the Constitution. There have to be very weighty reasons for departure from this rule. Otherwise, it may disturb the equilibrium by making many direct recruits junior to such ex-servicemen even when such direct recruits joined the services in civil posts much earlier than the ex-servicemen. Thus, an exceptional category carved out for giving such a benefit only to those who were commissioned in armed forces during war time could not be extended to each and every ex-serviceman merely because he has served in armed forces.

Videos & Tv Shows On Law & Exim

List of some important videos & TV shows on Law & EXIM by Adv. Jayprakash Somani on his YouTube Channel 'Jayprakash Somani EXIM & Legal'

Legal Videos: Hindi -English

1) SLP in Supreme Court / Special Leave Petitions in the Supreme Court of India

2) Transfer of Civil & Criminal Cases by the Supreme Court of India / Transfer of Matrimonial Cases

3) Appellate Jurisdiction of the Supreme Court of India

4) Jurisdictions of the Supreme Court of India

5) Public Interest Litigation in the Supreme Court of India / PIL in Supreme Court

6) Article 32 Writ Petitions in the Supreme Court of India

7) Bail Matters Top 10 Supreme Court Cases

8) FIR Quashing in High Court & Supreme Court

9) Bail & Anticipatory Bail Matters in Supreme Court

10) Insolvency & Bankruptcy Matters in the Supreme Court

11) Insolvency & Bankruptcy Code 2016 Part 1

12) Insolvency & Bankruptcy Code 2016 Part 2

13) Insolvency & Bankruptcy Code 2016 Part 3

14) Corporate Liquidation Process

15) Supreme Court Rules & Procedures Webinar of 2.5 hour on Zoom

16) RDDBFI Act, 1993 (Introduction)

17) The Indian Contact Act 1872

18) Negotiable Instruments Act (Introduction)

19) How to avoid matrimonial disputes& some more videos

20)SEBI Matters in the Supreme Court

21) Matrimonial Matters: Supreme Court's 20 Case Laws

22) Consumer Matters Supreme Court's 20 Case Laws

23) Service Matters Supreme Court's 20 Case Laws

24) How to Search Lawyer for Your Matter

25) Property Matters Supreme Court's 20 Case Laws

26) Bail Matters: Supreme Court's 20 Case Laws

27) Supreme Court / High Court Vacation Benches

28)69000 Teacher's Recruitment Matters of UP Government in the Supreme Court

29) Contempt of Court Matters in the Supreme Court

30) Advocate Act's Matters in the Supreme Court

31) Business Law Matters in the Supreme Court

32) Banking Matters in the Supreme Court

33) Labour Law Matters in the Supreme Court

34) Arbitration Matters in the Supreme Court

35) Careers in Law -Zoom Webinar by Adv. Jayprakash Somani

36) Civil Matters in the Supreme Court

37) Consumer Protection Act | Consumer Matters in the Supreme Court

38) Corporate Matters in the Supreme Court

39) Criminal Matters in the Supreme Court

40) Role of Respondent in the Supreme Court of India

41) Motor Vehicle Accident Matters in Supreme Court with case laws

42) Article 131 Original Suits in Supreme Court

43)PIL in Supreme Court/ Public Interest Litigations in the Supreme Court of India'

44)CAB Citizenship Amendment Bill is not Unconstitutional

45) Supreme Court of India Cases & Process – Marathi

46) Legal Services Export / Export of Legal Services

47) Transfer of Matrimonial Cases by the Supreme Court of India

48) Public Interest Litigation PIL

49) The Specific Relief Act (Introduction)

50) Corporate Insolvency Resolution Process CIRP

51)ABMM's Career 5 - Careers in Law

52) Transfer of cases by Supreme Court

53) Writ Petitions in High Court & Supreme Court of India

54) Supreme Court Jurisdictions - Appeals, SLP, Writ Petitions, Transfer, Original, Review, Curative

55)LEGAL INDIA TV Show: Cases Handled in Supreme Court

56) Corporate Liquidation Process

57) Legal Services Export / Export of Legal Services

EXIM Videos: Hindi -English

1) Yes, I can do Import Export Business Easily! 36 points excellent video in Hindi

2) Yes, I can do Import Export Business Easily! 36 points excellent video in English

3) Import Export Business – Hindi video

4) Import Export Business - English video

5) Export Import Marathi TV Interview

6) Scope for Commerce Students in International Business- TV Show

7) Scope for Management Student in International Business- TV Show

8) Scope for Engineering Students in International Business – TV Show

9) Women in International Business- TV Show

10) How to do Import Export Business Successfully!'

11) Where one can get full information on Import Export Business?

12) What to do import & export?

13) Import Export Workshop/ Training/Course/ Diploma

14) How to Start Import Export Business & How to grow it. Live Webinar

15) Success Stories & Failure Stories in Import & Export Business

16) For MSME Scope in Export & Import...

17) Exports In Agri. & Food Products – English & some more videos

18) Exports to Dubai, Aabudhabii. e. UAE

19) Jewelry Exports from India

20) How to attend EXIM workshop to become excellent Exporter

21) Import Export Best Training Course – Online & Offline

22) Agri Product Export

23) Scope for Woman in International Business

24) Management Graduates Scope in International Business

25) Pharma Product's Export

26) Best Import Export Course | Practical Training | Aaronica Global Exim

27) Import Export Business for Commerce Graduates

28) How Do I Get Export Orders? Finding International Buyers

29) What Is APEDA In Import Export Business?

30) Which Is The Best Product To Export From India?

31)EXIM Remark by Manoj Kumar Faridabad

32)EXIM Remarks by Mahesh Telangana

33) What Licenses I Need To Start Import/ Export?

34) How Can I Increase My Import Export Business?

35) Which Is Best B2B Website For Import/Export Business?

36) Export Import Management with Global Marketing

37) How to Start Export Import Business | 51 Points Video

38) Scope for Commerce & Other Graduates in International Business

39)BE A SUCCESSFUL EXPORTER FOR OUR NATION - Marathi video

40) Export of Textile , Cotton, Agri., Food, & other products & services

41) Exports from MP, CG, MH, GJ & CA in Fresh Fruits & Vegetables

42) Exports in Agri. & Food Products- Hindi

43) Start your Online/E-Commerce Business

44) How to Start Export Import Business & Grow it

45) Exports in Textile & Other Products

46) Start and grow EXIM business - Live English Webinar

47)'Import Export Business!' Why, Who, What &How can one do it easily!!

48) Live: Export of Product & Services During & After Lock Down Period

49) Frauds in Import Export Business

50) Import Export for Business Man

51) Import& Export for Women

51) Import& Export for Graduate & Post - Graduate Students

52) Agriculture Exports from India

53) Digital Marketing Setup - Marathi

54)2nd Secret of Successful Businessman

55) Digital Marketing Set up

56) Legal Services Export / Export of Legal Services

57) Export& Import with UAE

58) Service Exports / Exports by Service Providers

59) Import Export Workshop/ Training/Course/ Diploma

60) Exports& Imports with USA

61) Selection on Product for Export

62) Top Products Exported from India

63) What to do import & export?

64)ABMM Career 2 - 'Careers in Business & Industries

65) How to do Import Export Business Successfully!'

66)5 Secrets of Successful Businessman

67) Export from MP, Chhattisgarh &Vidarbha Nagpur

68)EXIM Hindi - Textile & Apparel Export

69)EXIM Hindi - Export Import Practical Training In Delhi, Kolkata, Mumbai and Pune

70) Import Export Business

71) Import Export Business Hindi

72) Import Export Business English video

73) Import Export Business Marathi

74) Women in International Business by Exim Guru Adv. Jayprakash Somani

75) Opportunities in Foreign Trade- Adv. Jayprakash Somani's special interview

ÞÞÞ

List Of Adv. Jayprakash Somani's Books

1. Supreme Court of India's Leading Case Laws on 'Insolvency & Bankruptcy Code 2016'

2. Bail Matters – Supreme Court's Latest Leading Case Laws

3. Arbitration Matters- Supreme Court's Latest Leading Case Laws

4. Property Matters - Supreme Court's Latest Leading Case Laws

5. Matrimonial Matters- Supreme Court's Latest Leading Case Laws

6. Election Matters- Supreme Court's Latest Leading Case Laws

7.SEBI Matters- Supreme Court's Latest Leading Case Laws

8. Banking Matters- Supreme Court's Latest Leading Case Laws

9. Service Matters- Supreme Court's Latest Leading Case Laws

10. Contempt of Court Matters- Supreme Court's Latest Leading Case Laws

11. Consumer Protection Matters- Supreme Court's Latest Leading Case Laws

12. Corporate Law- Supreme Court's Latest Leading Case Laws

13. Supreme Court's AOR Exam- Leading Cases

14. Armed Force Tribunal - Supreme Court's Latest Leading Case Laws

15. Acquittal From 376 - Supreme Court's Latest Leading Case Laws

16. Negotiable instrument – Supreme Court's Latest Leading Case Laws

17. Contract Act- Supreme Court's Latest Leading Case Laws

18. Insider trading- Supreme Court's Latest Leading Case Laws

19. Foreign Exchange and Management Act- Supreme Court's Latest Leading Case Laws

20. Income Tax Act- Supreme Court's Latest Leading Case Laws

21. Company Law- Supreme Court's Latest Leading Case Laws

22. Competition & Monopoly Matters- Supreme Court's Latest Leading Case Laws

23. Compassionate Appointment- Service Matters- Supreme Court's Latest Leading Case Laws

24. Compulsory Retirement- Service Matters- Supreme Court's Latest Leading Case Laws

25. Voluntary Retirement- Service Matters- Supreme Court's Latest Leading Case Laws

26. Seniority- Service Matter- Supreme Court's Latest Leading Case Laws

ÞÞÞ

These Books are available online at

1. **Notion Press:** https://notionpress.com/author/jayprakash_somani
2. **Amazon:** https://www.amazon.in/s?k=jayprakash+somani
3. **Flipkart:** https://www.flipkart.com/search?q=Jayprakash%20Somani

ÞÞÞ

Printed by Libri Plureos GmbH in Hamburg,
Germany

List Of Adv. Jayprakash Somani's Books

1. Supreme Court of India's Leading Case Laws on 'Insolvency & Bankruptcy Code 2016'

2. Bail Matters – Supreme Court's Latest Leading Case Laws

3. Arbitration Matters- Supreme Court's Latest Leading Case Laws

4. Property Matters - Supreme Court's Latest Leading Case Laws

5. Matrimonial Matters- Supreme Court's Latest Leading Case Laws

6. Election Matters- Supreme Court's Latest Leading Case Laws

7.SEBI Matters- Supreme Court's Latest Leading Case Laws

8. Banking Matters- Supreme Court's Latest Leading Case Laws

9. Service Matters- Supreme Court's Latest Leading Case Laws

10. Contempt of Court Matters- Supreme Court's Latest Leading Case Laws

11. Consumer Protection Matters- Supreme Court's Latest Leading Case Laws

12. Corporate Law- Supreme Court's Latest Leading Case Laws

13. Supreme Court's AOR Exam- Leading Cases

14. Armed Force Tribunal - Supreme Court's Latest Leading Case Laws

15. Acquittal From 376 - Supreme Court's Latest Leading Case Laws

16. Negotiable instrument – Supreme Court's Latest Leading Case Laws

17. Contract Act- Supreme Court's Latest Leading Case Laws

18. Insider trading- Supreme Court's Latest Leading Case Laws

19. Foreign Exchange and Management Act- Supreme Court's Latest Leading Case Laws

20. Income Tax Act- Supreme Court's Latest Leading Case Laws

21. Company Law- Supreme Court's Latest Leading Case Laws

22. Competition & Monopoly Matters- Supreme Court's Latest Leading Case Laws

23. Compassionate Appointment- Service Matters- Supreme Court's Latest Leading Case Laws

24. Compulsory Retirement- Service Matters- Supreme Court's Latest Leading Case Laws

25. Voluntary Retirement- Service Matters- Supreme Court's Latest Leading Case Laws

26. Seniority- Service Matter- Supreme Court's Latest Leading Case Laws

ᑭᑭᑭ

These Books are available online at

1. **Notion Press:** https://notionpress.com/author/jayprakash_somani
2. **Amazon:** https://www.amazon.in/s?k=jayprakash+somani
3. **Flipkart:** https://www.flipkart.com/search?q=Jayprakash%20Somani

ᑭᑭᑭ

Printed by Libri Plureos GmbH in Hamburg,
Germany